When the CROWN CRACKS

28 Doable Devos for When Life's Not a Fairy Tale

Loveland, CO

When the Crown Cracks...
28 Doable Devos for When Life's Not a Fairy Tale

Copyright © 2015 Sophia Joy

Visit our websites:

group.com
group.com/women

Unless otherwise indicated, all Scripture quotations are taken from the *Holy Bible*, New Living Translation, copyright © 1996, 2004, 2007, 2013 by Tyndale House Foundation. Used by permission of Tyndale House Publishers, Inc., Carol Stream, Illinois 60188. All rights reserved.

ISBN 978-1-4707-2309-5

Printed in the United States of America.

10 9 8 7 6 5 4 3 2 1   24 23 22 21 20 19 18 17 16 15

Dedicated to my mom, who has helped
me repair and polish my crown through
the craziness of life, and to Pastor Ray, my
biggest cheerleader through pain and fear.

In the midst of devastation, heartache, and loss,
simply putting on your lipstick and claiming a crown
doesn't seem to work the same magic it did on those
days that were filled with sunshine and rainbows. After
all, life was great; you were rolling around the kingdom
like you owned the place. Life wasn't perfect, but it was
filled with blessings, and you had no reason to question
your royal status.

Then one day—out of that same blue sky—lightning
strikes and it isn't long before the storm clouds and rain
block out any flicker of the sunshine that so recently
warmed your heart. In that darkness it's easy to feel
your crown slip or crack. Often it feels more like
it's ripped from your hair and hidden in the tangled
undergrowth of pain.

Princesses aren't supposed to get hurt, right?

How much simpler life would be if only that were true.
However, the strongest princesses I know have felt
intense pain. A husband in perfect health one day, and
paralyzed from a mysterious illness 48 hours later. A
marriage torn apart by infidelity and alcoholism. A child
lost to a heart defect. Cancer.

All these princesses experienced great pain, suffering,
and loss. They also grew moment by moment to trust
God's plan and, in retrospect from the safety of God's
loving arms, they learned to appreciate the growth
from the struggle.

Although it isn't always easy to remember to run to God when you're struck with the onset of tragedy, it is vitally important. We tend to reason that "Pain doesn't feel good, and God is good, so God really shouldn't have much to do with it other than making it stop. What else would a loving God do?"

In actuality, these trying moments are huge boulders that God has allowed to roll in your direction. Boulders that can either push you snug up against God's chest, held so tight your nose is stuck right up in his hairy armpit, or drive you so far away that trying to draw close to God seems like climbing Mount Everest.

Sweet princess, I wish there was something I could write in this book to instantly take away your pain, confusion, and frustration—but there is nothing like that to be written. Instead, this book will offer you a daily safe space to explore your feelings, offer comfort, and encourage you through challenging times—directing you to the loving arms of God.

Each day you will look to the CROWN to find those loving arms. After all, any royal knows the crown is the defining accessory.

Please know that you are amazing and wonderful and that sometimes God places people in your life to help you through challenging events. If at any point your feelings are overwhelming and you feel you may be an endangerment to yourself or others, call a professional counselor, therapist, or hospital right away.

When the
CROWNCRACKS...

Keep Your Eye on the C.R.O.W.N.

Each day as we see what God has in store for us we'll be focusing on our C.R.O.W.N.

Comfort

A select verse from the Bible to show how much God cares about you and wants to hold his daughter through this challenging situation.

Respect

A princess with a cracking crown needs to respect herself, her feelings, and especially her God.

Outward Thinking

The simplest way to make your life seem a little easier is to lend your hand to someone else, claiming at least a moment to remember life exists outside your struggle.

Workout

Physically release some stress while giving yourself a natural high from an elite endorphin rush.

Nutrition

Pass over the bon-bons. It's time to focus on foods to improve your mood and claim your princess pride.

Comfort

When the comforts of royal life are snatched away and you're left hoarse from shouting from the tower for your prince to come to your rescue, it is good to know there are words for such an occasion tucked away in the Bible. This book of God's Word is filled with verses of comfort, hope, encouragement, and peace.

It's easy to want to believe that your princess status leaves you exempt from pain and suffering. That promise simply isn't there. Instead, verse after verse offers comfort in times of pain, leading us to believe that God expects our lives to have painful moments. Wait a minute. I'm a princess, daughter of THE King. Why would God expect a royal like me to experience darkness and discouragement? Much like the princess tormented by the pea beneath layers and layers of mattresses, modern-day princesses just like you need a struggle to see the pure intentions truly in your heart. When hardships enter into our lives, our true character and center of life will come into focus.

For some this may be an unexpected bump in the road that will quickly come to pass, while for others it could be an ever-deepening moat ready to swallow you whole with no end in sight. The verses found in the Bible do not minimize the challenges we experience. Sometimes life stinks, and there may not be a Bible verse that can change that fact. What it can change

When the CROWNCRACKS...

is your *response*. It can offer hope in something bigger than circumstance.

That doesn't mean God wants us to have those painful moments. However, we are humans living in a world full of other humans lending itself to the opportunity to be disappointed and empty.

The good news is God is with you, and he will use our human mistakes for the good of those who love him.

Each day will bring an inspiring verse. Take time to meditate on it. Read it more than once. Ask God to use the verse to speak to your heart, heal your wounds, and bring you a comfort no person can offer.

Respect

Respect is a key component to surviving struggle; especially respect for yourself and for God.

Pain, hardship, and suffering work their evil ways by planting seeds of doubt. What easier way for evil to win than to make you think you're the problem—or better yet, that maybe God is the problem.

The princess that illustrates this perfectly is Princess Elsa of Arrendale (you remember her from *Frozen*—right?). As a child she finds her magical gift to create snow and ice wondrous and playful. But this gift turns devastating after a single accident that injures her sister. Despite the joy the ability brought Elsa and her sister, Elsa is asked to hide her gift. The resulting pain and fear is bigger than the possibility of good that could have blossomed out. Elsa has become the problem and is isolated from the kingdom.

It's tempting for us to travel the same path as Elsa. A broken relationship or lost job definitely twists the knife into the heart of our ego, deflating the momentary value of worldly worth. At times we may even wish for a poisoned apple to speed along the inevitable pain. Sickness and loss of life point the finger at the God of the universe who can stop everything in its tracks if he so wishes. The problem with this line of thinking is that it leaves out the fact that God both knows how the story ends and God is the writer of our stories. He may not enjoy seeing us struggle, but he can see past this moment and open our eyes to God's eternity and plan.

In times of struggle it is challenging, at best, to remember how wonderful you are and how awesome and intricate God's plan is. But it is also a most excellent time to truly examine your heart and ensure that God is at the center. To remember that the blessings of life that come and go and cause joy and pain are just life's blessings rather than the meaning of life. That your cup is full with just you and God, and that everything else fills your heart to overflowing in order to share that love with the world.

As you mend your broken crown, you will take time each day to focus on recognizing where your heart truly is and the feelings you are experiencing. You'll be encouraged to make God your foundation and center and to evaluate the truth of your feelings. You'll spend time in reflection that even the magic mirror may envy as you open your eyes to your continued value and God's unending love, even amidst evil queens and glass coffins.

While princesses are not immune to pain, despair should not enter their kingdoms. Recognizing the difference can be hard. Pain can be intense and overwhelm you for long moments, but focusing on the strength of God being enough can be the tiny, little ray of sunshine that will eventually part the clouds— revealing the blue sky of peace.

Outward Thinking

What you feed grows.

No, we aren't talking nutrition just yet. Rather, this is a simple explanation reminding you that the place you devote your energy to will become a bigger part of you and your life.

When life feels like it's crumbling around you, it's too easy to replay every second in your brain, thinking maybe there is a way you could have prevented the pain.

When you concentrate solely on the hole in your life, it starts to look bigger. Then, at some point, you can't help but stick your finger in the hole and poke around because it bothers you so much. Next thing you know, the hole is bigger, and it's even harder not to think about it.

Compare it to a beautiful painting that you lovingly created. You admire it…yet are not satisfied with the result of the little bush in the foreground. It has a spot on it that you tried to turn into a cheery bird, but that didn't work and now every time you look at the painting, all you can see is an ornery, short bush with a blue blob that steals the attention from the rest of the canvas

You may be tied up in knots gazing at this beautiful work of art, because despite the vast beauty, the only thing you see is failure and pain…until you let yourself focus on the rest of the painting. Once you can accomplish that, the spot seems a little smaller. Trust me, it's still there, and it will probably be the first thing you see for a long time, but it doesn't have to consume your masterpiece—or you.

In the Bible, God says in Isaiah 58:10, "Feed the hungry, and help those in trouble. Then your light will shine out from the darkness, and the darkness around you will be as bright as noon."

He is providing the answer to escaping pain and sadness. Reach out to others. Your life circumstances may seem insurmountable at the moment, but they are still not the only problems in the world. Each day you will be challenged to look outside yourself at the world around you and the people in your life that could use encouragement, comfort, and help. As you are forced to reach beyond your problems to your princess heart, you will be renewed to see the light that is within you offering hope and peace.

Workout

Have you ever wondered why the princesses in fairy tales never stay in bed for three days without showering or changing clothes and probably not brushing their teeth? Not only does it make a very uninteresting story, it also does no good whatsoever. When you hear the evil queen wants you dead, you go for a run through the forest and are lucky enough to meet seven little men that you can cook and clean for. That definitely sounds like a happily ever after escape, right?

Perhaps not. But, getting outside and moving will make you feel better. Science says so.

Aerobic activity—the kind that gets your blood pumping and showing a princess glow while still able to talk—promotes several responses in your body that help improve your mood. First, it controls cortisol levels. Cortisol is a hormone that your body releases in response to stress. It's great for escaping danger but not so great for replaying the moment your stepsisters crushed your dreams for a night out. Also, exercise releases endorphins, another hormone that improves your mood and reduces the perception of physical pain.

Another benefit to adding activity is to embrace a healthy sense of control. At times struggles can feel immensely chaotic and increase stress simply because we feel like we no longer have a grip on what happens in life. By dedicating about 20 minutes a day to an exercise routine, you can experience a sensible amount of control over one aspect of your day. Be careful not to go overboard, however. Princesses will find no peace being a control freak.

You will notice the focus on aerobic activity. This is because studies have shown that 20 minutes a day can be effective in treating mild depression and possibly anxiety. Some of the days will also include reflective practices to improve breathing. When you feel down, often your breathing becomes shallow, which then continues the cycle of not feeling great as you're not getting as much oxygen as your body craves. The breathing exercises will help you to focus only on breath for 10 to 15 minutes, improving your sense of peace and your clarity of mind.

The suggested activities are relatively simple, so feel free to do more if you are up for it. Do what feels comfortable. Just make sure to get out and do something.

As always please consult a doctor if you haven't exercised recently or if you have any specific medical concerns.

Nutrition

Food can be at the heart of any princess problem. Depending on the degree of the pain or the problem at hand, food can feel like a huge comfort or it can be revolting to think about. The primary concern as we examine nutrition while correcting your crown is to make healthy choices, using food choices to help heal rather than create more hurt.

Many foods will help perk up a princess. Throughout your journey to repair your crown you'll focus on adding foods that contain nutrients shown to help ward off depression and improve your mood.

Some of these foods include omega-3 fatty acids, B vitamins, tryptophan, serotonin, and antioxidants. Omega-3 fatty acids may help to boost mood when they are converted into an anti-inflammatory hormone. B vitamins such as folic acid and B6 may be helpful in treating mild depression and increasing the efficacy of prescription anti-depressants. Tryptophan is an amino acid that helps create serotonin, a neurotransmitter that offers positive feelings and a state of calm. Several different antioxidants are also suggested as they help to reduce inflammation and promote communication between the gut and the brain.

Why do you want your digestive tract and your brain to talk? Many neurotransmitters and hormones are formed in the digestive tract. If your gut is happy then your brain is happy. You've probably noticed the opposite association if you're nervous about something and need to run to the bathroom quickly. Thankfully, adjusting your diet should be easier than a mad dash.

Again, don't get crazy with control. Rather, focus on including healthy options to help you feel better. A princess might as well give herself the right fuel to rule the kingdom once the witch finally gives up.

C—Tears

"Jesus wept." (John 11:35)

God loves you just because you are. It might be hard to believe, but anything you do can't make him love you more. He sent his Son to die just for you. What more do you need to believe how much he loves you?

R—Write It Out

There are places to write in this book each day. Or you can find a journal or an old notebook you can use to record your thoughts throughout this journey. Writing your thoughts is a great, healthy outlet for all the emotions stuck inside you. Whenever you have things you want to say to a person or you have a situation that has stolen your crown, write it down. The simple act of releasing words to paper can at least momentarily ease your pain. If you're not sure where to start, simply write how you feel.

I feel _____ .

Notice the period. Don't try to analyze why you feel how you do or what is making you feel that way. Stop with how you feel and leave it at that. Just take the first step to owning your emotions.

O—Write a Note

You are a blessed princess. Even when it feels like everything in your world is crumbling, you have blessings surrounding you. In order to see them, you have to shift your focus to the things that encourage you. Today think of one person you are grateful to have in your life. Now write that person a note (one that requires a stamp is super special), thanking him or her for their role in your life.

The person I'm writing a note to is…

W—Walk It Out

Take the opportunity to get outside, hopefully in the sunshine, and walk. Look at the beauty around you and let it soak into your soul. Open up your heart and talk to Jesus as your blood begins to flow. If you need to, let the tears flow as well.

N—Write It Down

Fill in the following food diary, paying special attention to your emotions when you are eating. For many of us, times of distress can result in eating too much or too little, both which have negative effects on our bodies. Don't worry about changing anything you eat yet. Later we will focus on adding foods to help improve your mood.

What I ate.	How I was feeling when I ate it.

Thoughts from Day 1

_____

_____

_____

_____

_____

_____

_____

_____

_____

_____

_____

_____

_____

_____

When the
CROWNCRACKS...

C—Joy

"So you have sorrow now, but I will see you again; then you will rejoice, and no one can rob you of that joy." (John 16:22)

No one can get around momentary pain and sorrow. It happens to the best of us—sometimes when we don't even see it coming. But rest assured, when you can lift your head out of your sorrow and see Jesus' loving gaze you will have a joy that can't be taken away.

R—It Happens

Part of grieving the pains of life is recognizing the fact that the tragedy has happened. You do not need to know why it has happened—you may never know—but you do need to let reality sink in. Use the space below to describe what stole your sparkle. Don't try to rationalize why—simply state the facts. There is a time to attempt to learn from things; now is not that time.

O—Support Sorrow

Recognize that other people also experience sorrow. Whether you think their troubles are larger or smaller in comparison to your own, understand that they hurt, too. Consider someone who is currently going through a challenging time and reach out. Make a phone call, meet for coffee, or go for a walk together. Simply get together and focus on supporting that person in their sorrow rather than lamenting on your own.

W—Kick Sorrow's Behind

Hopefully by now, it's been established that pain and suffering hurt. (As if it actually needs to be taught. You're in it…you know it all too well.) Sometimes it hurts so badly you just want to punch something. Well, go for it. I would not suggest actually punching something unless you're in a gym with heavy bags hanging from the ceiling, but the act of making a punching motion in the air can let out similar aggression and frustration. Make sure your feet are set one foot slightly ahead of the other with a little bend in your knee. Hold your tummy in tight, and use the strength of your hips and the twisting of your waist to pummel that pain into next week. Keep it up for 10 to 15 minutes, and you should be breathing hard but feeling a little lighter.

N—Another Day of the Food Diary

Yes, another day of writing down everything you eat. Remember it's just as important to record your emotions throughout the day, too. Having this information on paper will help improve your habits as you continue this journey and not just blame a bad day for your food diary.

What I ate.	How I was feeling when I ate it.

Thoughts from Day 2

_____

_____

_____

_____

_____

_____

_____

_____

_____

_____

_____

_____

_____

_____

_____

When the CROWNCRACKS...

DAY 3

C—Strong Arms of Comfort

"The eternal God is your refuge, and his everlasting arms are under you." (Deuteronomy 33:27)

When you feel trapped in circumstances, look no further than the strong arms of Jesus holding you, waiting patiently to offer comfort.

R—Own Your Emotions

Feelings are not bad. Even bad feelings aren't bad. There are ups and downs in every fairy tale—that's part of what makes the stories exciting, even if it can be painful prior to the final kiss. The problem arises when you put on your princess smile, continuing your elbow-elbow-wrist-wrist wave to the approving audiences, and constantly pretend you are not falling to pieces inside.

Life right now may simply stink. It's okay to feel that way. Take a moment to write your emotions—no justification necessary. Simply limit yourself to how you feel. This is your chance to recognize your feelings and to let your princess hissy fit loose.

O—Pick Up a Park

It may be hard to find a woodland forest full of animals waiting to be your newfound friends, but certainly you can find a green space that needs your love. Focus your attention on beautifying the world around you, starting as simply as tending to the local park. Grab a bag, some gloves, and that princess power to inspire your kingdom. Pull a few weeds, pick up a bit of trash, and see the world a little brighter.

W—Walk the Park

While completing the royal duty of cleaning up the left behind trash of others, take some time to enjoy the surroundings of nature as you walk. Pick up the pace for an extra 20 minutes, and watch your princess glow grow.

N—Food Diary. Last One!

Tracking diet is not necessarily glamorous, but it does offer a glimpse into how you are taking care of your royal temple. Write what you are eating and how you are feeling for one more day, then evaluate the last three days for anything that jumps out at you. Are you eating too little? Shoving chocolate in your face instead of crying? Examine what is motivating you to eat and the choices you are making.

What I ate.	How I was feeling when I ate it.

Thoughts from Day 3

_____

_____

_____

_____

_____

_____

_____

_____

_____

_____

_____

_____

_____

_____

_____

When the CROWNCRACKS...

C—The Lord Is With You

"Do not be afraid or discouraged, for the Lord will personally go ahead of you. He will be with you; he will neither fail you nor abandon you."
(Deuteronomy 31:8)

Although it may be easy to fear and become frustrated when life is raining poisoned apples, find comfort in knowing that the Lord is not only with you, but ahead of you. He knows everything that is coming your way and will not leave you disappointed once this struggle is behind you.

R—Get Honest With God

Let's face it. God already knows your thoughts. It does no good for you to think otherwise or to try to go through the motions of saying the things good people who love God should say when you're not sure you believe it. God is big. He can handle your fears and doubts. The way to rid yourself of these feelings is to admit it and hand it over to God. Dig deep into your heart and ask yourself if you believe God is personally with you, he will not fail you, and he has not abandoned you. If you find that you're not completely sure, tell him and ask him to help you overcome this doubt and show you his presence in this pain.

Write your thoughts to God here:

O —Pet a Poodle

It doesn't have to be a poodle. Simply visit a pet store or an animal shelter and spend at least 10 minutes with one of God's furry creatures. Animals often offer an unconditional love and understanding of emotion that our human friends sometimes struggle to reach. As humans we want to fix the problem, while sometimes all we need is to sit and pet a puppy and feel love that comes at no cost of our own. Remember that God loves you the same way—with no requirements, simply where you are.

W—Princess Power Jacks

Jumping jacks are okay for a court jester, but a princess wants to kick it up a notch. To put some power in your jumping jack, push your arms up and swing them around in a wide circle away from the midline of your body while jumping up and doing a mini splits. This is even more fun on a trampoline if you can find one. Do 20 seconds of joyous jumping, then take a 10 second break. Repeat for 3 to 4 minutes, then add 20 minutes of cardio however you'd like (walk, trot, jog, bike, or whatever you like!).

N—Drink It Up

Water. It's an essential component to a healthy lifestyle and especially so during stressful times. Dehydration on its own can lead to fatigue and depression, which is definitely not helpful while awaiting your escape from your tormented tower. Drinking plenty of water can stimulate positivity and increase memory, perhaps pointing to your route out.

Thoughts from Day 4

_____

_____

_____

_____

_____

_____

_____

_____

_____

_____

_____

_____

_____

_____

_____

_____

C—Delight

"He led me to a place of safety; he rescued me because he delights in me." (Psalm 18:19)

Focus on the second part of this verse. God delights in you. The God of the universe delights in you exactly as you are. There are no standards you must reach before his delight can take over your life. Hold that delight close to your heart, and as you do, you will feel his gentle guidance to the place of safety.

R—A Jewel Among Jewels

You are that jewel. Your value in no way reflects what your life looks like at this moment. It's easy to fall into believing the lies that say if you were valuable and loved then this wouldn't be happening. Those are lies. The comforting verse today (and many others) shares that the Lord himself delights in you. There is no use in allowing yourself or the world around you to talk you into anything else. You are awesome. God says so. Reflect and write your thoughts on your value and any stumbling blocks you may foresee attempting to trip you into believing the deception.

O—Phone a Friend

It's time to talk. As you process the events occurring in your life, sometimes it's easy to get stuck in your head; or worse yet, stuck in your life whenever you talk to another human soul. Today your challenge is to phone a friend and genuinely ask him or her about their life or anything they need to talk about. This conversation is not about you. If they ask about your current struggle thank them for their concern, but acknowledge that you called because you want to hear about their life and offer your support.

W—Slow Down and Breathe

Meditation can be a wonderful way calming your mind and turn your focus to God. But let's face it—when the fairy tale is upside down, it's hard to clear your mind. This is when it may be helpful to meditate on a Bible verse. Today continue to read and repeat to yourself the credo from Psalms or another favorite verse while breathing deeply. If other thoughts creep into your mind as you're meditating, push those thoughts out and focus on the verse. Focus on this for 10 to 15 minutes.

N—Cut the Coffee

Caffeinated beverages such as coffee may reduce serotonin levels, which helps produce feelings of happiness and satisfaction. Therefore if you're sad, can't eat, and live off the eight cups of coffee brewed each morning, you are building an uphill battle to feeling good again. Try replacing your caffeinated drink with water and a twist of lemon or a sprig of mint to ignite your energy.

Thoughts from *Day 5*

_____

_____

_____

_____

_____

_____

_____

_____

_____

_____

_____

_____

_____

_____

_____

_____

C—Come Close to God

"Come close to God, and God will come close to you."
(James 4:8)

Can it really be that easy? When you're in the midst of the battle for the kingdom of your heart, you have a choice—get closer to God or pull away. Find comfort in knowing that as you get closer and place your trust in God, he will be close to you. It may take time to feel that closeness, but one day you will wake up knowing the suffocating squeeze of pain has been replaced with the tight embrace of protection and love.

R—Search Your Soul

Pain and challenge provide an excellent opportunity to search the truth of your soul and recognize what is your priority. Ask yourself out loud (or better yet, have a friend ask), "What is most important to you?"

Is it more important that your current circumstance change or to have God grow in your heart? This is a hard question to ask. There are many great gifts God has given us that we love—relationships, health, financial security—but they are only gifts. If they become more important in your life than God himself, then perhaps an interruption to that priority is the gift you never knew you needed.

Write your answer to the question "What is most important to you?" here:

0—Closet Transformation

Time to get to work and clean out your closet. The princess with the most shoes is not necessarily the happiest princess. Empty out anything you haven't worn in the last year and take it to a donation site in your community, so another princess can enjoy them. Let each item you pack away also release a layer of the emotion your princess pride clings to.

W—Full Body Crunch

The core of a princess must be strong emotionally, spiritually, and physically. Lie on the floor, and bring your knees toward the midline of your body while lifting your shoulders off the floor. Be sure to breath and not strain your neck (having to wear a cervical collar on an injured neck could distract from your tiara!). Do 20 repetitions, take a break, and repeat two more times. Add 20 minutes of cardio for a great workout.

N—Get Close With Chocolate

That is correct. Your nutrition challenge for today is to eat chocolate, preferably dark chocolate. Not only does chocolate tantalize your taste buds, it's rich in magnesium which reduces anxiety and tryptophan that is needed to create that magical happiness found from serotonin. Take the time to relish your three ounces as you claim your royal right to chocolate.

Thoughts from Day 6

_____

_____

_____

_____

_____

_____

_____

_____

_____

_____

_____

_____

_____

_____

_____

_____

C—Believe

"Jesus told him, 'Don't be afraid; just believe.'"
(Mark 5:36, NIV)

In the busyness of keeping up the kingdom, many end up complicating life more than necessary. Take Jesus' simple message to heart. Do not be afraid. Just believe.

R—God's Got It

Not only do princesses complicate the kingdom, but they also try to control it. When life is not the fairy tale you have imagined and orchestrated, it's easy to question everything you've done to influence where you are and everything you could do to get it back to where you want life to be. Being a proactive princess can be beneficial, but some things in life are not under your control. Recognize which things you are not able to change, and let God handle it. He's a big God who can take care of more than you imagine. Write exactly what you are releasing to God to remind yourself to let go when you begin to grab the tails of dragons.

O—Princess Pick-Me-Up

Write a princess pick-me-up offering encouragement to a friend. It doesn't have to be long, eloquent, or even rhyme. It's important for you to remember there are others in the kingdom who need the help of the King. Pass on your encouragement and watch your own comfort grow.

Here's the name of the friend I'm going to write encouraging words to:

_____

W—Fear Not the Burpee

If there is any routine callisthenic that is more feared than the burpee, I'm unaware of it. Have no fear! This is a fantastic full body exercise any princess can add to her routine.

Begin standing in a neutral position. Quickly bend your knees to a squat, bringing your hands down to the floor, just in front of your feet.

Jump or step your legs back so you are in a plank position...

Then immediately jump your feet back to your hands.

Stand up, reaching your hands overhead and jumping up to touch the sky.

That's one!

Repeat 10 times. Rest and try to repeat four more sets throughout your day.

N—Purple Potatoes

There is no easier way to look fear in the eye and try something new than purple potatoes. A familiar flavor and pleasing to the eye, these colorful potatoes contain anthocyanins, a special antioxidant that decreases inflammation and potentially increases happiness.
Roast or grill with a little olive oil and garlic to create a mood-boosting side to your evening meal.

Thoughts from Day 7

_____

_____

_____

_____

_____

_____

_____

_____

C—Choose Courage

"Wait for the Lord; be strong, and let your heart take courage; wait for the Lord!" (Psalm 27:14, ESV)

God's timing is often not the same as your timing, leading to plenty of waiting. But while you are waiting, this verse encourages you to be strong and to let your heart take courage. The word "let" implies that this is something you get to decide to do. You can let your heart take courage or choose to let your heart live in fear. Where would you rather wait?

R—Be Brave

Finding courage in your heart is probably easier said than done. Courage requires you to face your fear head on, acknowledging it and loosening its powerful hold on your heart. What fears do you need to face? How will these give you new opportunities to embrace courage and strength? If you are struggling with letting go, ask God for help. He's kind of into that whole saving mankind thing.

Write about those fears here, then talk to God about how you can be brave in facing them—together.

0—Classy Compliment

Today's task may require courage for some royals. Get out of your head, and look around your world for someone that is doing something great or looking fantastic and tell them. Offer a compliment to a friend, co-worker, or stranger, making sure it's a compliment that is from a sincere heart. Watch their face light up with appreciation, and remember how simple it is to positively impact someone's day.

W—Corpse Pose

Don't let the creepy sound of this position sway you. Instead know that it will be easy to wait for the Lord in this position. The corpse pose is a position that is basically lying on your back in a relaxed position. Allow your legs to rest in a neutral position, and put your arms at your sides with your palms up. As you hold the pose for up to 10 minutes, rest your eyes and focus on your breathing, relaxing as much of your body as you can. (This is a great position to pray in!)

N—Honey, Honey

You are already sweet, so there is no need to add more sweetness to your day, but you're going to do it anyway. Add a bit of honey to your tea or toast, and savor the flavor. The simple taste of something sweet offers a soothing touch to your mood. Plus there are antioxidants called polyphenols in honey that improve health. Some studies show that eating honey improves your memory and reduces anxiety. Sweet!

Thoughts from Day 8

_____

_____

_____

_____

_____

_____

_____

_____

_____

_____

_____

_____

_____

C—Go Higher

"From the ends of the earth I call to you, I call as my heart grows faint; lead me to the rock that is higher than I." (Psalm 61:2, NIV)

As you continue to call for God's help in your time of struggle, remind yourself where you would like to be led. There is a rock that is higher than you and will bring you great comfort.

R—Let Go of Yourself

In order to be led to a higher rock, you must first recognize that you are not the highest hill in the kingdom. Let go of yourself, the outcome you desire, and the control to which you cling. While many princesses have excellent plans and are ready to serve as advisory council to the King, remember that God is greater than even you, sweet princess.

Take a moment to examine how you rank yourself and your plan compared to God and his plan. Jot your thoughts about this here:

0—Prayer Rock

Find a smooth stone to place under your pillow. It should be large enough to feel as you lay your head down at night. You will probably want to clean it so as not to dirty the royal sheets, and you may choose to paint it or write an inspiring verse on it. When you sneak up to slumber and bump your head, let this rock remind you of the higher rock and call to God to lead you there.

W — Jump Higher

This princess is ready to catch some air. Find a box or landing that is large enough and sturdy enough for you to jump onto and land safely. Ready? Explosively jump from both feet onto your box and jump back down. Repeat 10 times, take a break, and do three more sets. Add some cardio at the end, and feel great!

N — Excellent Eggs

Scrambled, fried, poached, or even as "Toads in a Hole" — eggs are an excellent mood booster. They offer protein, vitamin B, and omega-3 fatty acid — all which work to increase your feelings of well being and help to optimize your body functions.

Thoughts from Day 9

_____

_____

_____

_____

_____

_____

_____

_____

_____

_____

_____

_____

_____

_____

C—Peace

"Don't worry about anything; instead, pray about everything. Tell God what you need, and thank him for all he has done. Then you will experience God's peace, which exceeds anything we can understand. His peace will guard your hearts and minds as you live in Christ Jesus." (Philippians 4:6-7)

These two verses pack a lot of princess punch for the weary royal. It is nothing short of fantastic how God tells you what to do rather than just leaving it at "don't worry." God is anxiously waiting for you to talk to him about whatever it is that's concerning you. His offer in return? Peace. Peace that blows your mind. He may not take out his fairy godmother wand and fix the situation, but he will give you the peace that makes no sense to anyone but carries you through.

R—Forget the Why

It's so easy to get stuck in wanting to know *why* you are experiencing this particular pain. Perhaps you feel that knowing the complete picture will make it okay to let go of the pain enough to feel at rest. Trying to find good in struggle, lessons to learn from bad choices, or how this experience can be used in the future is not a bad thing. But keeping you focus on the "why" or the lesson to be learned can become a bad thing when it takes our focus off of God.

The credo verse today shares that God is the only source of a comfort beyond understanding—nothing you can hear or deduce from hours of analyzing will bring you more comfort. It also suggests focusing on thanking God for what he has done. Do that here—write a list of things you're thankful for and focus on that instead of the "why."

O—Royal Field Trip

Your visit may not be announced with horns and white stallions, but it will be appreciated. Visit a local children's hospital or a nursing home. Bring a stuffed animal, balloons, or flowers, and ask who needs a visitor. If this is outside your princess comfort zone, simply ask to leave your gift at the desk for a staff member to deliver. If you're feeling bolder, visit in the room, and share a smile with someone who may also benefit from a kind heart on display.

W—Snooze

Whether it's Snow White or Sleeping Beauty, it's obvious that beauty sleep is important to any princess. For a princess who is handling extra stress, the beauty from super sleep is more than skin deep. Your body requires sleep to recharge. That's both your physical body and also your emotional state of being. Climb into your royal chambers a bit early tonight, and do your best to catch up on zzz's you might be missing.

N—Princessy Pistachios

Every princess should go nuts on occasion, and it doesn't have to be a public display of craziness. Popping a handful of pistachios into your mouth may help to reduce stress. No need to go crazy and eat the whole bag, but one and a half ounces should do the trick.

Thoughts from Day 10

_____

_____

_____

_____

_____

_____

_____

_____

_____

_____

_____

_____

_____

C—Hope and Joy

"I pray that God, the source of hope, will fill you completely with joy and peace because you trust in him. Then you will overflow with confident hope through the power of the Holy Spirit." (Romans 15:13)

You get to choose if you want to worry, fret and fear, or trust God. Joy and peace come only through trusting God and the power the Holy Spirit offers.

R—Where's Your Hope?

Where you expel your energy is often where your hope lies. Take a moment and ask yourself where your thoughts are throughout the day. Are they imagining a life without the current struggle you're dealing with? Do you constantly hope for a relationship to reconcile, a job to come, or a baby to arrive? It's not bad to hope for these things. Every princess pines for her prince and an orderly kingdom. However, a confident hope in Jesus must be greater than everything else. Ask yourself what is most important to you—a relationship with Jesus or whatever other desire is on your heart.

Write your thoughts on this here:

0 — Wave at Children

Elbow, elbow, wrist, wrist. Get used to it. This is the
royal wave practiced across the lands from the time you
were a little lass yourself. Pretend you're in a parade
today as you wave at children everywhere. If you're
driving by—wave. If you see them at play—wave.
See a bus full of kiddos? Wave! You can wave at
grownups too, but children are more apt to allow joy to
escape their hearts and let it shine onto their little faces,
bubbling that joy into your life.

W — Joyful Activity

The point of exercise is to get moving, create new energy, and release endorphins to help you feel better. Today think back to any activity that brings joy to your heart, and do it for 20 minutes. Perhaps you need to unleash your inner dancer, bike through trails like you did when you were ten, or even play tag with your friend or child. It's much more fun to sweat through laughter. Let yourself enjoy the moment.

N — Joyful Juice

Make a special concoction of juice, fruit, and ice to slip smoothly past your princess lips, turning your pout into pleasure. The antioxidants in fruits help control inflammation while the natural sugars present bring a pleasant smile to your face. Try juicing two apples, two carrots, and a handful of spinach—or any combination that sounds tasty to you. Enjoy!

Thoughts from Day 11

_____

_____

_____

_____

Thoughts from *Day 11*

_____

_____

_____

_____

_____

_____

_____

_____

_____

_____

_____

_____

_____

_____

_____

DAY 12

C—Dampen Discouragment

"Why am I discouraged? Why is my heart so sad? I will put my hope in God! I will praise him again— my Savior and my God!" (Psalm 43:5)

Discouragement and sadness are not traits that reveal hope in God. Of course even princesses will have moments where you feel like you'd rather be in the dungeon since that's how you feel anyway. But don't make up your bed and decorate the walls in that gloomy place. Hope in God means trusting his goodness and his hand in your life.

R—Replace Your Thoughts

There are so many amazing things about your brain, but one is that you can't think two thoughts about the same thing simultaneously. What that means is you can't think "apples are poisonous" and "an apple a day keeps the doctor away" at the same time. Yes, you can think them back-to-back, but not at the same time.

For today, challenge yourself to replace any negative thoughts of discouragement, pain, and sadness with a thought of hope in God and all he is capable of.

Thoughts I want to replace—and what I'll replace them with:

O—Movie Date

Plan a movie date with a friend tonight. Sometimes your brain just needs a distraction from the thoughts that creep up. Choose a comedy, make some popcorn (hold the butter), and let yourself laugh.

W—Never-Ending Stairs

Find a staircase and start stepping. Do this even if the only stairs you can find in your kingdom are two steps— just continue stepping up and back down. As you step, focus on positive messages such as today's credo or other Bible verses or a worship song you love. Keeping the positive messages from God in your mind forces the negative thoughts from your head. Plug your headphones into the royal workout mix and resolve to step away from negative thinking.

N—No More Blueberry Blues

Enjoy a half-cup of fresh blueberries today. Not only are they tasty little orbs of nature's sweetness, they're packed with antioxidant compounds that increase cognitive function and decision making.

Thoughts from Day 12

_____

_____

_____

_____

_____

Thoughts from *Day 12*

_____

_____

_____

_____

_____

_____

_____

_____

_____

_____

_____

_____

_____

_____

_____

C—Taste and See!

"Taste and see that the Lord is good. Oh, the joys of those who take refuge in him!" (Psalm 34:8)

Yes, God gave you chocolate and that is one reason you can rest assured that God is good, but don't get caught up in just tasting that God is good. Focus on the second part of the verse, reminding you of the joy found in taking refuge in God. You get to choose every day, every moment, if you want to battle on your own or from the comforting arms of Jesus.

R—Marvel God's Majesty

There is joy to be found in the refuge of Jesus. Look around today and find things in your world that reflect how majestic he is. It could be a bouquet of flowers, a beautiful sunset, mountain peaks, ocean waves, a flower surviving the concrete jungle, a kind face in a crazy supermarket. The list is endless. Take time to see how amazing God is today.

List a few of the things you've noticed:

0 — Smile!

Yes, princess, that's all you have to do today.
Simply allow yourself to smile, relaxing enough to
enjoy the moments of goodness in your day. Feeling
the joy of Jesus will only help you through the
heaviness of life's circumstances.

W — Power Skip

One of the great joys of youth is skipping—so why not give it a princess pick-me-up? A power skip is jumping while you skip. Lift your right knee toward your hip, and reach your left arm over your head, jumping as high as you can off the ball of your foot. Land safely and switch legs. Skip for 20 seconds, take a 10 second break, and repeat for 3 minutes. Round it out with your 20 minutes of cardio.

N — Enjoy Edamame

Today's treat is tasty soybeans packed with tryptophan, which helps build the happiness-boosting neurotransmitter serotinin. It's even more fun if you eat them out of the shell with a little salt. There is something about unwrapping your gift of food along the way that makes a princess heart happy.

Thoughts from Day 13

_____

_____

_____

_____

_____

_____

_____

_____

_____

_____

_____

_____

_____

_____

_____

C—Glory

"Yet what we suffer now is nothing compared to the glory he will reveal to us later." (Romans 8:18)

Delayed gratification is something many of us struggle to appreciate, yet God promises something so great that we won't even remember what was so bothersome once we reach that glorious eternity.

R—Ten Grateful Things

God's glory and goodness is not reserved for the heavenly realms; it exists in your current kingdom, too. Sometimes it's harder to see past the moat keeping you captive, but that doesn't mean your blessings aren't there. Can you walk, move, and breathe on your own? Do you have food on your table every night? A roof over your head? A friend with a kind, listening ear? Look around your world and list ten things for which you are forever thankful.

1.

2.

3.

4.

5.

6.

7.

8.

9.

10.

O—Friendly Field Trip

The world around you is a testimony to God's glory. Grab a princess pal and take a field trip to the most beautiful place you can think of. (It needs to be a place you can get to today, so don't be disappointed if you can't make it Machu Picchu.) While you're at your delightful destination, take time to soak it in and to ponder the amazing creation of God. Remember you are the crown of that creation made in God's image with more care and intention than any other wonder of the world.

W—Focused Breathing

Breathing may not seem like a workout, but it is important to your physical and emotional well-being. Sit or recline in a comfortable position so you can simply breathe for ten minutes. As you concentrate on your breathing, breathe in slowly through your nose for five seconds, hold your breath for five seconds, then release your breath slowly out your mouth for five seconds. You should feel at least a little more calm and refreshed.

N—Whole Grains for a Whole Lotta Happy

Throughout the day enjoy a serving of whole grain. This could be beautiful brown bread to make a sandwich, some brown rice with your dinner, or a yummy granola bar. Keep in mind, however, that whole grains shouldn't look as fair as Snow White's skin. The darker and more complex grains will assist in a steady release of serotonin throughout the day.

Thoughts from Day 14

_____

_____

_____

_____

Thoughts from Day 14

_____

_____

_____

_____

_____

_____

_____

_____

_____

_____

_____

_____

_____

_____

_____

When the CROWN CRACKS...

C—God's Grace

"Three different times I begged the Lord to take it away. Each time he said, 'My grace is all you need. My power works best in weakness.'" (2 Corinthians 12:8-9)

It is not a new thing to feel like you continually ask God for something and receive a response different than hoped for. Here is confirmation that God may know it's more important to learn to rely on him in your weakness than to hope for a fairy-godmother to save the day in a poof of the magic wand wonder.

R—You Are Loved…Continually

You may feel you're constantly asking for God to show up on his white horse, ready to save the day. But perhaps he looks more like an ogre in your eyes today, and you're missing the love God's waiting to share with you. Remember, even though God's love for you may not look the way you want it to at this moment, it is there in abundance even in the muddy swamp. Every time you see yourself in a mirror today, rather than asking who is the fairest, remind yourself that you are loved exactly for who you are and where your life is right now.

Write a message to yourself here, reminding yourself of God's love—and write it again in lipstick on your bathroom mirror so you're sure to see it!

O—Love Three People

As your love bucket gets filled up today, it's natural that you'll feel compelled to splash some love on others. Find three people to show love to today. It could be as simple as opening a door for someone with their arms full, offering a flower, sending a note, or sharing a meal. What matters most is spreading the love.

W—Three Minute Abs

Every princess feels better with a strong core. Complete the following 3-minute abdominal routine for a quick fix to feel the burn. Push yourself for each of the following crunches, remembering to exercise your abs and not lift with your neck.

Center crunch—Lay in a relaxed position on the floor with your knees bent and feet resting on the floor. Lift from your abdominals until your shoulder blades come off the floor for 30 seconds.

Right Crunch—Still lying on the floor, bring your right ankle across your left leg. Lift your left shoulder toward your right knee for 30 seconds.

Left Crunch—Now bring your left ankle across your right leg. Lift your right shoulder toward your left knee for 30 seconds.

Leg Lift—Lift your feet off the floor and hold them straight in the air directly above your hips. Gently lift your feet up, raising your princess booty off the ground for 30 seconds.

Bicycle—While lifting your shoulders off the ground, bring your right knee toward your head, and push your left foot away. Try to touch your left shoulder to your right knee. Then switch sides, pushing your right foot away and bringing your left knee toward your head and right shoulder toward your left knee. Continue alternating for 1 minute.

When the CROWN CRACKS...

N—Boost of Broccoli

Enjoy some beautiful broccoli during your day today—
either raw or steamed. Feel the power of omega-3 fatty
acids running through your body and nourishing your brain.

Thoughts from *Day 15*

_____

_____

_____

_____

_____

_____

_____

_____

_____

_____

_____

Thoughts from Day 15

_____

_____

_____

_____

_____

_____

_____

_____

_____

_____

_____

_____

_____

_____

C—Trust

"Commit everything you do to the Lord. Trust him, and he will help you." (Psalm 37:5)

It sounds pretty easy. Trust God and he will help you. Keep in mind, it doesn't promise how God's help will look, but God will help as you learn to trust him.

R—Committed?

Commitment is a big thing. You may know a prince or two that has chosen the life of a frog on his bachelor pad rather than run away with the fair maiden. However, commitment can bring comfort and security knowing the love and trust in a relationship will be there forever.

What are you most concerned with in your life—getting your way or doing it God's way? Take 10 minutes to reflect on where your commitment is contained. Jot your thoughts here.

0—Random Act of Coffee

While carrying out your princess duties today, buy a coffee or maybe even lunch for a random person. Pay for the person behind you in line, or at another table in the restaurant, or bring a free beverage or meal to someone you see. You don't even need to see how they respond to feel the warm fuzzies of helping one of God's children because you're pretty much doing it for the Lord, right?

W – Inchworm

Sometimes a princess may appreciate a reminder that the little things in life can also be committed to God; even tiny inchworm moves. Start standing straight and tall. Slowly bend over keeping your legs as straight as you can until your fingers touch the floor. Then, keeping your abs tight, walk out to a plank or push up position. Take tiny steps back to your hands and continue four to six times. Add some cardio when you are through, too!

N – Salmon

This pretty pink fish is packed with omega-3 fatty acids that may boost your mood, ease some pain, and clear your brain. Enjoy a four-ounce serving with your lunch or dinner and some brightly colored veggies for a super food addition to your day.

Thoughts from *Day 16*

_____

_____

_____

_____

_____

_____

_____

_____

_____

_____

_____

_____

_____

_____

C—Talk to God

"The Lord hears his people when they call to him for help. He rescues them from all their troubles. The Lord is close to the brokenhearted; he rescues those whose spirits are crushed." (Psalm 34:17-18)

Rest assured, God is close to you. In moments when you are brokenhearted and crushed in spirit, it can be harder to feel it. That is why it's so important to continue talking to God, asking for his help and comfort.

R—Recruit a Cheerleader

Rah Rah Ree...Encouragement is a blessing and a great reminder that God is with you. If no one has stepped up with her princess pom-poms yet, ask a friend to commit to cheering you along through this process. Make sure this is a loving, Christian friend who will encourage you to trust and persevere through this challenging time of life.

My cheerleader is...

_____

O—How Are You?

How are you? What a simple question. However, how often do you ask someone this question and not even stick around to hear the answer? Today as you go about your day, take time to ask at least three people how they are—and wait for their complete answer.

W—Squat Jumps

You may need a cheerleader or at least some encouragement to finish your exercise today. It's worth it—a strong princess doesn't happen waving out the royal window.

Start by standing tall. Squat down to a normal squat position with your booty back, feet flat on the floor, and knees no further than your toes. Then, jump and reach your arms to the sky. Do 10 times. Rest and repeat three more times. Keep smiling...and continuing your cardio too.

N—Greek Yogurt

This may be the food of the mythological Greek gods. Overflowing with protein and probiotics, Greek yogurt provides some of the essential building blocks to creating a healthy digestive tract and the neurotransmitters than make you smile. You may want to be mindful of fats and sugars while picking your princess treat today, but there are plenty of great options for a scrumptious snack.

Thoughts from *Day 17*

_____

_____

_____

_____

_____

_____

_____

_____

Thoughts from Day 17

_____

_____

_____

_____

_____

_____

_____

_____

_____

_____

_____

_____

_____

_____

C— Enduring the Trials

"Dear brothers and sisters, when troubles of any kind come your way, consider it an opportunity for great joy. For you know that when your faith is tested, your endurance has a chance to grow. So let it grow, for when your endurance is fully developed, you will be perfect and complete, needing nothing."
(James 1:2-4)

This has been my personal theme verse for many years. Troubles becoming joy is a crazy concept to appreciate when life can only be described as chaotic. I've found that the times when you can't make sense of the disaster around you and the only thing left is faith that God has it covered is the time when character and faith bloom.

R–Joy in Trouble

This may be one of the more challenging activities. Think of one joy that is present or coming in your current struggle. Some tragedies are so big that you don't want to consider any joy resulting, but God says clearly to consider the possibility. Simply opening your mind to the wonderment of God's work in your life brings some comfort. Note your thoughts on this here:

O—Chores for a Friend

Rather than letting your mind sink to places that make you feel like you have little to offer, focus on a tangible way to help a friend today. Call up a friend and offer to play Cinderella for an hour doing dishes, vacuuming, or running errands. If she declines your offer, find a sneaky way to do something kind for her anyway (pull weeds while she's at work!).

W—Timed Trials

Nothing says "fun exercise" like an obstacle course. You may feel less goofy if you bring a friend along to complete this activity, but it can be done on your own. In the backyard, at a park, or even at the gym, set out an obstacle course jumping over sticks, running around bushes, or climbing a slide. See if you can beat your time each time you complete your race. After 20 minutes, you'll not only feel the burn but also the possibility of joy in trials and obstacles.

N—Go Bananas!

Not only are bananas a gorgeous yellow hue that brightens anyone's day, they also boost tryptophan, the building block for serotonin, which helps the happy mood. For a great treat, smoosh and blend a frozen banana until smooth, adding a little peanut butter to make a great ice cream alternative.

Thoughts from *Day 18*

_____

_____

_____

_____

_____

_____

_____

_____

_____

_____

_____

_____

_____

_____

_____

_____

C—God's Strength

"I know how to live on almost nothing or with everything. I have learned the secret of living in every situation, whether it is with a full stomach or empty, with plenty or little. For I can do everything through Christ, who gives me strength."
(Philippians 4:12-13)

Many of us want to be strong enough to get through any situation, forgetting that we need God's strength when we are out of our own. When we ask for and utilize God's strength, we can attempt to look from his perspective and to find comfort in any situation—despite it not matching the plans we envisioned.

R—Finding God's Strength

Unless you happen to moonlight as a superhero, you can probably think of a time when you've needed God's strength to carry you through a challenging situation. Take time to remember that time of your life and reflect on how you felt throughout the struggle and once you were on the other side of the rainbow. God has helped you in the past and will continue to be there now and always. Write your reflections here:

O—Strength for a Stranger

Believe it or not, you're not the only princess in your kingdom that could use some extra strength right now. Look around today, and see whom you could offer strength. If you're comfortable, buy one flower for a stranger, and see their eyes light up, realizing they are worth your dollar. Perhaps someone needs your physical strength to carry groceries to the car or the strength of a comforting smile or conversation. Keep your heart open to how God wants to use you today, and follow through.

W—Jumping Jack Planks

Today you get to dig down and find your strength within. Jumping jacks are a great cardio exercise, and planks offer a fantastic strength challenge for the whole body. So why not put them together? It only makes sense. Hold your body in a plank position with your shoulders above your wrists, and be on your toes with a straight line from your head to your heels. Now pop your legs apart like a jumping jack while holding your upper body and core strong. Do 10 repetitions, take a break, and repeat three times.

N—Content With Chamomile

Cozy up with a cup of chamomile and reflect on God providing strength for you when you feel you have nothing left. The calming chamomile should help find your contentment as you let God's strength seep into your soul.

Thoughts from *Day 19*

_____

_____

_____

_____

_____

_____

_____

_____

_____

_____

_____

_____

_____

_____

C — Comfort and Cheer

"I cried out, 'I am slipping!' but your unfailing love, O Lord, supported me. When doubts filled my mind, your comfort gave me renewed hope and cheer."
(Psalm 94:18-19)

When you're slipping, remember to cry out to the Lord. It doesn't matter if it's because you chose to wear those cute heels instead of hiking shoes or if it's because someone took a hose and made your mountain a slippery mess that you wanted no part of. God is your support and your comforter. He can renew your mood and help you smile in the most unlikely of circumstances.

R — Big Girls Don't Cry...Or Maybe They Do

It's time to let it all out. Find a safe space with someone who loves and supports you, or lock yourself in the royal restroom and let yourself cry. It is okay. You don't have to be strong enough to get through every circumstance. In fact, over and over in the Bible God reminds you that he wants to be your strength. Let yourself cry and give your pain to God. He will take care of it. Then you can continue through the day knowing your Father, the God of the universe, supports you. Write your thoughts about this here:

O — Say a Little Prayer

You're not the only one crying. It's tempting to get caught up in your struggles, talking about them constantly, thinking about them even more, and leaving no room in your life to care about what's going on in the lives of others. It's time to change that. Cry out to God on behalf of someone else. It may be someone you know, a stranger on the street, or a friend of a friend. Dedicate several minutes to praying for this person. Ask God to give them hope and joy in the midst of their circumstances.

𝒲—Climb the Rope

Don't worry. It's an invisible rope, so it will be hard to slip (and hopefully you're not stuck in a tower anyway!). Lie with your back on the floor with your knees bent and feet on the floor. Now imagine a rope hanging down just before your knees, and climb hand over hand as you lift your torso off the ground. Try to lift for eight counts before you climb back down. Repeat five times, and then enjoy some cardio.

𝒩—Tart Cherry Juice

The tantalizing tartness of this cherry juice won't make you cry, but rather renews your body with powerful antioxidants to fight free radicals in your body and sharpen your mind. Sip a glass and feel refreshed!

Thoughts from Day 20

_____

_____

_____

_____

_____

_____

_____

_____

_____

_____

_____

_____

_____

_____

_____

C—You Are Valuable

"What is the price of five sparrows—two copper coins? Yet God does not forget a single one of them. And the very hairs on your head are all numbered. So don't be afraid; you are more valuable to God than a whole flock of sparrows."
(Luke 12:6-7)

Say that again—don't be afraid. You are valuable. You may have forgotten your value or even started to believe you must lack value because of your circumstances. The events of life are not an indicator of your value. Instead, the fact that God chose to create you reflects your value. The sparrows do nothing to earn God's love and provision for life and neither do you. Do not be afraid. You are valuable.

R—Five Valuable Traits

Think of your five most valuable traits—yes, there truly are five wonderful and valuable things about you! Ponder the gifts that create the amazing person that is you. If this activity is hard for you, think of it as a thank you note to God, a celebration of gratitude. You're not allowed to stop until you have at least five traits recorded, but feel free to record more.

1.

2.

3.

4.

5.

O—Five Anonymous Notes

Get out five pieces of paper, and write out your favorite quotes, Bible verses, or encouraging phrases. Throughout your day drop these notes anywhere you feel a need; on a windshield in the grocery store parking lot, on the desk of the school teacher, a co-worker's computer screen, or a neighbor's front door. Everyone needs to be reminded of their value, so why not be a messenger of encouragement?

W—Five Rounds of Football Feet

It's time to get that valuable heart rate up. You've likely seen football players do a drill where they run through a path of tires. This is like that—but the tires are imaginary. With your feet shoulder width apart lift your feet off the ground, alternating feet as fast as you can. Keep up the frenzy for 20 seconds, rest for 10 seconds, and repeat for a total of five times. Of course, continue with your cardio as well.

N—Five Ounces of Chicken

Five ounces is a little larger than the standard four ounce portion, but we were having so much fun with the fives that we can add the extra ounce. Choose a seasoned kabob, a baked breast, or a portion hidden inside a noodle casserole. Chicken contains a good amount of tryptophan, one of the building blocks of the mood-booster serotonin.

Thoughts from Day 21

_____

_____

_____

_____

Thoughts from Day 21

_____

_____

_____

_____

_____

_____

_____

_____

_____

_____

_____

_____

_____

C—Be Glad!

"So be truly glad. There is wonderful joy ahead, even though you must endure many trials for a little while." (1 Peter 1:6)

God knows you will have challenges in this life. The measurement of "a little while" will vary from person to person and situation to situation, but the promise of joy ahead is the same. Allow gladness to creep into your pain and never stop expecting the hope and joy in God that lies ahead.

R—Gladness With God

A simple way to find some Jesus-joy is to spend time alone with God. The distractions (good, bad, and ugly stepsisters) can easily rob some of the joy and comfort that can only be filled by your Father. As you spend time alone today, empty your heart to God. Then be still, and quiet your mind so you may feel the love and joy in your heart.

After this time of quiet, write your thoughts here:

O—Joy Adventure

Get outside and walk, run, skip, ride your bike, or even do cartwheels while you explore the joy around you. Go at a pace you enjoy so that you may look around this wonderful world and see the little pieces of joy that God has placed to make your heart glad.

W—Wander With Wonder

Guess what? You may count your joy adventure as your workout today, just make sure to get in at least twenty minutes exercising your body and opening your heart. Twenty minutes of cartwheels isn't suggested, however, maybe stick to one or two here and there to perk up that smile.

N—Chew Gum

Any flavor will do, cinnamon, mint, or watermelon splash. Simply pop in a piece and enjoy. Not only does it remind you of the joy of childhood, it also has been shown to possibly elevate your mood. So, chew to your heart's content…with your mouth closed, of course; you're a princess.

Thoughts from Day 22

_____

_____

_____

_____

_____

_____

Thoughts from *Day 22*

_____

_____

_____

_____

_____

_____

_____

_____

_____

_____

_____

_____

_____

_____

_____

_____

C—Trust God

"Trust in the Lord with all your heart; do not depend on your own understanding. Seek his will in all you do, and he will show you which path to take."
(Proverbs 3:5-6)

It's easy to want to understand everything that's happening in your life. After all, it is your life. Yet sometimes God doesn't let you know the why; you simply have to concede that God is bigger than you and knows better than you. Trust God. Seek his will. Wait for him to show you the path.

R—God's Path

You're at a place where you're not sure you like where you're at. Or perhaps you feel like you're stuck. You want something different. Take some time to think on what it could mean to take God's path rather than your own. Write any concerns you may have in giving up control or redirecting a dream. God has it covered. Open your heart to it.

My reflections:

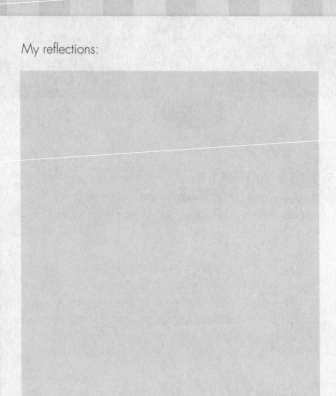

O – Walk the Path

Follow the path to your neighbors door and deliver a simple gift—some cookies, or apples, or granola bars, or even celery and hummus. Recognize the people around you that you may take for granted every day and let them know you care. Begin to appreciate God's infinite plan one person at a time.

W—Hit the Bike Path

Find a bike path, trail, or even a sidewalk to travel on for at least twenty minutes today. You don't have to decorate your bike with streamers and glitter to feel like you're the princess in a parade, but you would surely get noticed if you did. (And if you don't have a bike, walking is wonderful!) Enjoy your time on this short journey and release your thoughts, asking God to show you his path. Don't get frustrated if you don't see it today. He knows the right timing.

N—Avocados

Whether you're enjoying chips and guacamole, a turkey and avocado sandwich, or avocado and quinoa salad, including this delicious green addition should help bring a smile to your face. Not only is it super tasty, it is packed with serotonin, the mood boosting neurotransmitter we love.

Thoughts from Day 23

_____

_____

_____

_____

_____

Thoughts from Day 23

_____

_____

_____

_____

_____

_____

_____

_____

_____

_____

_____

_____

_____

_____

When the CROWNCRACKS...

C—The Gift of Peace

"I am leaving you with a gift—peace of mind and heart. And the peace I give is a gift the world cannot give. So don't be troubled or afraid."
(John 14:27)

These words from the mouth of Jesus tell you to not be afraid because he offers you a treasured gift. Peace of mind and heart. That means peace in what you are thinking and what you are feeling. More than likely, it will not make sense to the world and maybe even to yourself, but you can find comfort in knowing the peace that makes no sense is one that can stay with you as you struggle through any challenge.

R—A Bigger Peace

The life of a princess is busy and filled with many stressors and distractions. It's up to you to let go of those obstacles, opening your mind and spirit to the peace that is bigger than you can imagine. Peace from God himself.

Look for a quiet place, and talk quietly to God about the things for which you need peace. This isn't a magic spell. Jesus isn't going to show up dressed as the blue fairy. Instead, this is a chance for you to recognize what you need to let go, and then make every attempt to do so and experience a peace you couldn't imagine.

Write your thoughts and prayers here:

O—Peaceful Posies

Pick up a flower or a bouquet today and bring it home, putting it on display. As you look at these flowers throughout the day and week, remember the peace that God offers as he takes care of the flowers and even more so, you, his very own child.

W—Breath of Life

Without realizing it, you may be robbing yourself of peace with something as simple as shallow breathing. In the fast-paced world, your body naturally follows and often doesn't take a full breath unless you tell it to. Follow the instructions below for concentrating on full, peace of life, breaths.

Stand comfortably and inhale deeply as you lift your arms above your head. Hold your breath for 2 to 5 seconds, then exhale slowly while you lower your hands to your sides. Repeat 10 times. This works great for calming princesses of any age. Try this before and after your cardio today.

N—Peace in Caprese

Caprese salad or appetizers on a stick are a delicious way to get your peace on today. Gather tomato, natural mozzarella, and fresh basil leaves. Arrange them beautifully on a plate or kabob stick, and then drizzle with olive oil and add a touch of sea salt. The tomato contains a large amount of lycopene, a special antioxidant that reduces inflammation. Basil contains omega-3 fatty acids. Even the royals would enjoy this gorgeous dish.

Thoughts from Day 24

_____

_____

_____

_____

_____

_____

_____

_____

_____

_____

_____

_____

_____

_____

C – God's Purpose

"And we know that God causes everything to work together for the good of those who love God and are called according to his purpose for them."
(Romans 8:28)

The familiarity of this verse makes some princesses respond with a casual, "sure." Sometimes it doesn't feel like God knows what he's doing and he doesn't quite know what "good" looks like. We have such a limited viewpoint! Read how *The Message* translation paraphrases this verse:

"He knows us far better than we know ourselves, knows our pregnant condition, and keeps us present before God. That's why we can be so sure that every detail in our lives of love for God is worked into something good."

God knows you better than you know yourself. Can you trust him?

R—God's Got Good Plans

During your quiet time with God today meditate on the truth that God has good plans. It's often in the most unlikely, despairing situations that God works miraculous wonders beyond any fairy tale you've dreamed up. Write your thoughts and reflections about God's good plans here:

O—A Knowledgeable Friend

Call or visit the friend that you feel you know and love the most. Spend as long as you both have available in conversation, focusing primarily on what is going on in your friend's life. Do your best to focus on that person instead of the drama of your life. On your way back to your castle, ponder the fact that as much as you know and love this friend, God loves and knows you infinitely better.

W—Frog Jumps

This workout might help you attract a prince disguised as a frog—but it's likely you'll be too tired (and sweaty!) to kiss him! Start by squatting down with your hands touching the ground. Jump in the air as high as you can, landing in your previously assumed frog position. Keep it up for 10 jumps, then take a break. Repeat two more times or sprinkle them in throughout your cardio session.

N—Spinach Booster

Enjoy a serving of spinach today. Hide it in a smoothie (you really don't taste it), wilt it in your scrambled eggs, or savor it with strawberries in a salad. These gorgeous greens are packed with folic acid and vitamin B for your daily boost.

Thoughts from Day 25

_____

_____

_____

_____

_____

_____

_____

_____

_____

_____

_____

_____

_____

_____

_____

C—Passing Along Comfort

"He comforts us in all our troubles so that we can comfort others. When they are troubled, we will be able to give them the same comfort God has given us." (2 Corinthians 1:4)

You're working through your troubles and growing in faith and compassion. You can be sure that God will use your experience to help others around you, although you may not realize what a gift that is until someone needs your comfort.

R—Forgiveness

It is time to forgive. Perhaps you've already worked through forgiveness of a person that has wronged you, forgiveness toward yourself for making a bad decision, or even forgiving God for allowing pain in your life. If you haven't worked through this, it is time to get intentional.

Take time today to forgive whatever wrongs are holding you back from the open gift of love. This will be a process, as you'll more than likely have to forgive the same offense over and over in your heart until it no longer influences your day. It is worth the effort. Forgiveness offers the biggest gift to the forgiver.

Write your thoughts about this process here:

O—Look To Comfort

Look around your life—work, school, church, or your neighborhood—and find someone who needs comfort. It may be a simple smile or hug, or someone could need a coffee and conversation. Make yourself available to comfort someone else struggling, and be transparent in your struggles so that they may learn to follow the peace you've found in trusting God.

W — Flutter Kick

Your abs will be crying for comfort when you're done fluttering like a honey bee. Lie on your back, and lift your feet about 6 inches off the floor. You can put your hands under your princess booty if you'd like more stability. Now kick up and down for a minute holding your core tight. Don't forget the cardio.

N — Comfort Food

Oatmeal! For many of us oatmeal is a reminder of childhood. Of course, some princesses most appreciate an oatmeal cookie or breakfast bar. Feel free to enjoy your oatmeal in baked form or in a steamy bowl with a bit of brown sugar. Appreciate the steady release of serotonin the complex carbohydrate offers.

Thoughts from Day 26

_____

_____

_____

_____

_____

_____

_____

_____

_____

_____

_____

_____

_____

When the CROWNCRACKS...

C—Real Rest

"Are you tired? Worn out? Burned out on religion? Come to me. Get away with me and you'll recover your life. I'll show you how to take a real rest. Walk with me and work with me—watch how I do it. Learn the unforced rhythms of grace. I won't lay anything heavy or ill-fitting on you. Keep company with me and you'll learn to live freely and lightly." (Matthew 11:28-30, The Message)

Do you need rest? All princesses do! Find Jesus. Jesus is inviting you to come to him, to learn from him, and to rest in the comfort of his ways. Find your rest in the company of Jesus.

R—Rest With God

A princess may need her beauty sleep, but this isn't exactly a nap time activity. Rather, find a place where you can truly relax. You may want to leave the palace so there are fewer distractions like the dungeon full of laundry. Relax your eyes and your body. Listen for God. He knows your heart, and if you must empty it to him before you can relax, do so, but spend the majority of your time today resting in God's presence.

After your time of rest, note any words from God here:

O—Relax With a Friend

Call a friend and go for a relaxing outing. This could be a leisurely stroll around the park, a coffee on the couch, or a pampering pedicure. Remember, your focus is relaxing, so keep any tense conversation put away for today; it can take a day off.

W – Carry Heavy Burdens

This princess thinks any kind of lunge is a chore I'd trade with Cinderella any day. However, lunges are a powerful exercise that can increase your muscles and boost your booty. Find a space where you can walk about 20 yards. Take a large step, and lower to the ground until your back knee is nearly to the ground (or as far as you can comfortably go), then step through and repeat leading with the other leg. Make sure your front knee doesn't bend past your foot as this could cause injury to your knee. Continue this until you've gone all 20 yards. Then go back. Finish up your 20 minutes with a walk or jog. Great job, princess!

N – Go Nuts!

Most nuts—walnuts, almonds, pistachios, even peanuts—contain a significant amount of magnesium. Magnesium is great for calming muscles and reducing anxiety. Nuts are higher in fat, so don't eat a whole bag, but enjoy a healthy one-ounce serving.

Thoughts from Day 27

_____

_____

_____

_____

_____

_____

_____

_____

_____

_____

_____

_____

_____

_____

_____

_____

C—More, More, More

"Now all glory to God, who is able, through his mighty power at work within us, to accomplish infinitely more than we might ask or think. Glory to him in the church and in Christ Jesus through all generations forever and ever! Amen."
(Ephesians 3:20-21)

God can do infinitely more than you can even dream. He is the power that works inside you. Give God the glory and the space in your life to give you a glimpse at how your happily ever after in *his* kingdom can look.

R—More Than You Ask

You may have spent these last few weeks asking for God to do a lot in your life. You may be learning to let go of what you want and search for God's direction. Either way it's easy to come up with an idea of what you think it could look like.

Take a few moments to reflect on what could happen if you let go of the reigns of control and watch what God can accomplish with a willing servant. Continue to open your heart to the possibility of something greater than you can fathom. An eternity of happily ever after sounds better than Prince Charming on his white horse any day.

Write your thoughts about this here:

0 — Big Tip

In a last effort to let go, trust, and consider the implications of infinitely more than you can imagine. Go out to lunch, dinner, or coffee, leaving a tip for your server that's larger than you normally would offer. Really make this person's day! You may even feel inclined to pray for your server. Whatever is on your heart, follow it as you share simple joy today.

W – Mountain Climber

Dear princess, you have climbed mountains over the last few weeks. You should be proud of yourself, but before you pat yourself on the back, do a minute of mountain climbers.

On the floor with your hands under your shoulders in a push up or plank position, bring your right foot toward your mid-section while keeping your princess booty as low as you can. Switch feet, jumping or stepping, whichever pace is most comfortable for you. After a minute, finish out your 20 minutes of cardio, and celebrate your accomplishments and growth.

N – Tuna Dinner

Nothing says winner like a tuna dinner. You've worked hard, and now you can sit and enjoy a wonderful dinner or lunch. Bake it, make a tuna salad sandwich, or throw some albacore on your salad for a tasty treat packed with omega-3 fatty acids to feed your brain and boost your mood.

Thoughts from Day 28

_____

_____

_____

_____

_____

_____

_____

_____

_____

_____

_____

_____

_____

_____

_____

_____

When the CROWN CRACKS...

Congratulations!

You've completed your first 28 days of remembering your royal roots. By now, you should be learning that the circumstances of life do not define you. Your relationship with God, your Heavenly Father, is all that is needed to stake your claim on a happily ever after that lasts an eternity. The course of your life steers you closer to God and reliance on his grace and love.

Remember that no matter what dragons cross your path, towers hold you captive, or shrieking women taunt you with endless chores, you are loved.

No struggle diminishes that love.

No amount of time will cause that love to fade.

No person can tell you that love is not true.

No amount of guilt or shame or depreciation will ever change the fact that you are loved by the only King that has any power over the kingdom.

That King—the God of the universe—your Father, is there with you as you trust him now and learn to look for him in the future.

Even the fairy tale princesses had to go through challenges to reach their happily-ever-afters, and you are so much more than a storybook character.

You are God's precious jewel in the crown of God's kingdom.

Additional thoughts

_____

_____

_____

_____

_____

_____

_____

_____

_____

_____

_____

_____

_____

_____

Additional thoughts

_____

_____

_____

_____

_____

_____

_____

_____

_____

_____

_____

_____

_____

_____

Additional thoughts

_____

_____

_____

_____

_____

_____

_____

_____

_____

_____

_____

_____

_____

Additional thoughts

_____

_____

_____

_____

_____

_____

_____

_____

_____

_____

_____

_____

_____

_____

_____

_____